WESTERN STEAM DAYS REMEMBERED

No. 4079 *Pendennis Castle* heading an Ian Allan railtour. See pp. 55–6.

WESTERN STEAM DAYS REMEMBERED

An officer of the railway stands aside and affords full respect to No. 6029 *King Edward VIII* as the 4-6-0 sweeps majestically into Swindon in 1959. (Strathwood Library Collection)

Kevin Derrick

No. 7810 *Draycott Manor* at Lampeter. See p. 76.

This edition first published 2017

Amberley Publishing
The Hill, Stroud
Gloucestershire, GL5 4EP

www.amberley-books.com

Copyright © Kevin Derrick, 2017

The right of Kevin Derrick to be identified as the Author of this work has been asserted in accordance with the Copyrights, Designs and Patents Act 1988.

ISBN 978 1 9052 6981 6 (print)
ISBN 978 1 9052 6982 3 (ebook)

All rights reserved. No part of this book may be reprinted or reproduced or utilised in any form or by any electronic, mechanical or other means, now known or hereafter invented, including photocopying and recording, or in any information storage or retrieval system, without the permission in writing from the Publishers.

British Library Cataloguing in Publication Data.
A catalogue record for this book is available from the British Library.

Origination by Amberley Publishing.
Printed in the UK.

Contents

Preface	6
Introduction — Go West Young Man	7
Everyday Swindon	12
Sad & Decayed	17
Severn Bore	20
Western Rover	23
London Division	33
West Country Wanderings	41
Specials	51
Bristol Shiftwork	58
Swindon's Bone Yard	62
Preservation Movements	66
Cambrian Adventures	69
Interlopers	84
Ex-Works Swindon	90

Preface

Enthusiasm for the first two volumes of *Steam Days Remembered* has sent me back once again into the archive to make another selection of some of my favourite shots from the 1950s and 1960s in colour. This time around I have called upon another old friend to put some words together about his experiences as a younger man growing up with steam. Indeed you will glimpse a few similarities perhaps to your own memories of the time as we venture together through this collection into a bygone era.

Many readers will be familiar with the name of Peter Coton, who has been accredited to a number of previous releases in the *Sixties Spotting Days* series. These have been drawn from Peter's collection of colour slides, taken at a time when every month the railway periodicals announced a long list of freshly withdrawn locomotives – some are old friends, others not seen yet. But what of the man behind the lens, who is this fellow who, fortunately for those of us who were perhaps either too young, or too poor as schoolboys at the time, to have the money and equipment to take such shots – or even to be allowed by our parents to venture that far from our home town! As, sadly, far too many of the older guard of enthusiasts who were active at the time have now passed on, their photographic collections are sometimes preserved in a loft somewhere but more often forgotten about or, more tragically still, thrown out after a suitable period of mourning by the family. So we should give thanks to Peter and those others who took such shots and have been kind enough to allow us to see their work published today.

Kevin Derrick
Inverness 2013

A society visit to Swindon Works: the running shed, coded 82C, was blessed with warm early autumn sunshine on 24 September 1961, and respectfully dressed members were allowed to roam free to take their photographs. (Frank Hornby)

Introduction — Go West Young Man

When reminiscing about the past, you hope to strike a chord with others; to trigger their memories, invite challenges and stimulate debate. All of these, combined with the evocative illustrations that follow, lead to the seemingly endless fascination with the age of steam among those of us old enough to have seen at least some of its glory.

For the first few years after the war, my parents used to holiday in Looe, Cornwall. My first Great Western recollections date from 1950, when my father took me to Paddington, gave the guard 2s 6d and asked him to tip me out at Liskeard. I was to spend time with the young son of the owners of the bed-and-breakfast where we stayed. Sixty years later, you can wonder at many aspects of that alone: would you despatch a seven-year-old on such a journey on his own today; would the same guard 'work through'; would I be met at the far end, etc?

I was not yet at the 'spotter' stage, but the seeds were being sown. My only real memory of the journey was as the 45xx ran around the B set in the shadow of Moorswater viaduct. Standing at the open carriage window, I could see that the points were set for the line down to Moorswater shed, yet the clear sound of the loco coming towards me could be heard. In what I suppose was fatal fascination, I stood and waited for the inevitable derailment, and was amazed that it somehow didn't happen. And so my first experience of spring-operated points was learnt.

It was five years later that I noted down my first GW locomotive – No. 5055 *Earl of Eldon* – at the bufferstops at Paddington. I had finally badgered my parents into getting my first 'combined' ABC and could now do the job properly! Like many other lads, I regularly did a circuit of the London termini. My dad had a shop in Tunbridge Wells; he would give me a few shillings and off I'd go – the

Good fortune would smile upon No. 1420, seen at Leominster in March 1961, for preservationists rather than scrap dealers would win her tendering process after she was withdrawn in November 1964. (Strathwood Library Collection)

No such luck for 4300 Class Mogul No. 6381, seen at Hereford with a Gloucester service on 13 July 1963, just before the harsh thunderstorm struck with its withdrawal in November 1963 and scrapping seven months later. (Peter Simmonds)

9.01 'stockbroker's' train with a Schools to Cannon Street; Circle Line to Liverpool Street and the cavernous, sulphurous gloom there; and a regular anti-clockwise circuit to King's Cross, St Pancras, Euston and Paddington. I would end up at Waterloo mainline before going over to Waterloo East and catching the 16.20 from Charing Cross back home.

Paddington was always a delight. The locos were almost always clean and most of the tender engines were 'namers'; the ratio of named 'cops' was always best there. And my next memorable trip was a family holiday to the Isles of Scilly. We took the overnight train, but I declined a sleeper – there was much too much to miss! Details are long forgotten but some images endure, like that of the highly burnished Modified Hall, which left on a westbound parcels as folk tried to find their allocated sleeping compartments, and then wedge all their luggage in somehow. Later on, there was the unmistakeable silhouette of withdrawn Dukedogs at Swindon, awaiting their new career as razor blades. Funereal progress past Bristol and a re-acquaintance with the Modified Hall at Taunton, which had taken the more direct route via Newbury.

However, simply unforgettable was the climb out of Newton Abbot with the sight and sound of two locos attacking Dainton, the firehole doors open for a constant feed of fuel for the climb and the orange glow in the inky black of pre-dawn, accompanied by that indescribable music from the chimneys. Tiredness overcame me and I have virtually no recall after the Royal Albert bridge for the trip through Cornwall. A year later it was Mullion, involving a change at Gwinear Road and a trip down the Helston branch, and a further year on, Tenby. That one, beginning to mirror the pattern of post-war prosperity, was undertaken by road, but did not exclude a trip from Tenby to Pembroke Dock behind No. 7804 *Baydon Manor* and the discovery of where Neyland was!

My father was a picture-frame maker and we had an elderly customer, Miss Hithcock, who lived in Bath and would turn out charcoal sketches by the dozen, each of which were uniformly framed in 1-inch flat oak. It was worked out that it was cheaper (and more reliable) for me to carry her framed masterpieces down to Bath than to package them up securely enough to survive transit by any other means. And so it came to pass that I would be able to leave on the trusty 9.01 as the shop opened, get over to Paddington for the 'Merchant Venturer,' first stop Bath. Always a tip-top condition Castle turn, its punctuality was exemplary. A quick taxi ride and goods delivered and then it was back for the 14.10 stopping at Chippenham only, and this would get me on to the 16.20 from Charing Cross, due at Tunbridge Wells Central at 17.18, 12 minutes before closing time. What a good day's work – it probably accounted for a trip each school holiday until I was no longer eligible for half

A recent visit to the nearby works at Swindon has been afforded to one of the Churchward design of 2-8-0s at the turn of the 1960s. Another overhaul would be unlikely before being taken out of traffic in December 1963. (John Gill)

fares. One example of how locos were rostered for the same train, sometimes for months on end, was a homebound run behind No. 5066 *Wardour Castle*; the next time around it was the same loco, but renamed *Sir Felix Pole*.

August 1955 was long and hot, and no doubt I was an irritating little twelve-year-old. But my dad had a heart of gold and knew that I was relatively easy to entertain. One particular day he gave me a pound and said, 'Off you go then,' and, with riches beyond the dreams of avarice, off I went. You know the first and last legs already – but that particular day I abandoned the circuit of the Circle line and headed straight for Paddington and the 'Inter City', complete with a Stafford Road King at the sharp end. One stop at Leamington and there I am in Britain's second city, asking directions for New Street.

It was there that I bought my first copy of *Trains Illustrated*, with a Lord Nelson on the cover, and the news within that the first LMS Beyer-Garratts had been withdrawn. And while I can't recall which royal personage had taken me north, I will never forget my first run with a rebuilt Scot, No. 46162 *Queen's Westminster Rifleman*. I stood the whole way, stopping at Coventry only and with grit in my eye from Rugby onwards. My dad asked where I had been for the day and I think he was quite proud of my initiative. My mother was horrified!

Another visit to the running shed at Swindon on 16 October 1960 yields No. 7824 *Iford Manor* alongside No. 4969 *Shrugborough Hall*. (Frank Hornby)

Now in the last year of its six-year service life was No. 92220 *Evening Star,* put to work on the Bromford Bridge–Avonmouth Esso fuel train and pictured at Coaley Junction on 13 July 1964. (Gilroy Kerr)

So, as one year blended into the next, the writing was on the wall for steam, but no underlining for No. 5089 *Westminster Abbey*, which had remained for years the only one of the 5000 series of Castles that had escaped my gaze.

After the late 1950s, when Swindon had achieved so much good work adapting their fleet for the post-war austerities of poorer quality coal and the decline in maintenance standards, it was bordering on tragic to witness how the proud traditions evaporated. I guess the last stand by Swindon was their championing of hydraulic transmission for their diesel modernisation programme but, as successive Westerns emerged, you could tell the spark had gone and the names bore it out: Western Disaster,

On a sunny day in 1965, No. 4079 *Pendennis Castle* blows off from the safety valves as it runs easily on this day along the Down relief line at Twyford. (Strathwood Library Collection)

Introduction — Go West Young Man

What connoisseur of Western Region steam could walk past the ex-works Castle Class No. 7007 *Great Western* at Swindon on 28 May 1961 with a camera loaded with colour film, and not take an exposure in such lovely sunshine? (Late Norman Browne/Strathwood Library Collection)

Western Points Failure, Western Decline, etc. The glitter went out of the region, and locos were sent out in a condition that would have had shed masters of a few years previous hauled before the management and berated. We now remember the death throes of Western steam, the much-loved Brunswick Green that had been lovingly bestowed on almost everything now long buried beneath the muck and grime.

Three weeks after an epic high-speed run that set off behind No. 4079, 29 May 1964 saw a wonderful effort by a Modified Hall as its replacement, with further contributions from *Clun Castle* and *Earl of Ducie*. There were no 100-mph speeds as hoped, but I made one of my late pilgrimages to Old Oak Common. My long-time friend John Tiley was with me and shouted to me that there was something I ought to see inside the remaining roundhouse. My search for No. 5089 was over. She wasn't in the best of shape, working out her time from Oxley shed, and certainly not on class A duties. Nonetheless, the green paint shone through the patina of grime and the thoroughbred lines of the rebuilt Star were plain to see. John and I retired for a celebratory pint in the grotty little pub just up the road on the way to see if there was anything worth pointing a camera at on Willesden that day.

So, as 1964 morphed into 1965, Great Western steam finally gave up the ghost. The Kings had long gone and the handful of Castles reflected the attitude that now prevailed – No. 5042 *Winchester Castle* was bereft of safety valve bonnet, which was as embarrassing as the thought of your grandmother in the nude. The remaining Halls and Granges had bare patches on the cab sides where the number plates had been rudely wrenched off, spikes of steel that had once held nameplates and a pervading sense of decay and imminent death. Only *Clun Castle* relieved this awful period and the cancer of the lost spirit now transferred to the diesels, which would be plastered in an all-over blue and allowed to get as filthy as the steam they replaced.

So, in some way, it was almost a relief when the final fires were dropped and Great Western steam was taken out of its misery.

Peter Coton
Essex 2012

Everyday Swindon

A mix of 2-8-0 designs from Riddles and Collett mingle with a selection of Western Region express and mixed traffic 4-6-0s outside in the shed yard at Swindon on 24 September 1961, as society members make their way around 82C under the watchful eye of the shed foreman. (Frank Hornby)

One of the many 5700 Class pannier tanks built after Nationalisation in 1948 was No. 9680, built here in Swindon and released to traffic in April 1949. On 13 July 1963 it was finding employment with a Kemble stopping passenger service; with diesel multiple units taking over what services the Beeching cuts had left, work for such pannier tanks had all but dried up by December 1965, when No. 9680 was posted as withdrawn. (Peter Simmonds)

Even the pride of the Western Region, No. 6000 *King George V*, could not be kept spotless in everyday service with a light coating of ash, soot and dust adhering to the paintwork of this fine locomotive as it was moved out into the shed yard for the benefit of photographers. The much-prized souvenir bell from the engine's visit to the US for the celebrations of the centenary of the Baltimore & Ohio Railway in 1927 was always much polished, come what may. (Richard Icke)

A closer view of No. 7824 *Iford Manor* was also taken by our late cameraman on 16 October 1960. In another two months, the Charles Collett-designed Manor, which was among the last eight of her class released into traffic during December 1950, would celebrate its tenth birthday. Withdrawn in November 1964, it would be reduced to scrap by the end of February the following year – what a sad waste of resources by those responsible! (Late Norman Browne/Strathwood Library Collection)

Not exactly clean and pristine for its appearance at the head of the Cheltenham Spa Express, at one time the world's fastest train service, Castle Class No. 5084 *Reading Abbey* brings its rake of chocolate-and-cream Mark I coaches into the west end of Swindon with the Up service in 1959. (Strathwood Library Collection)

Works overhauls were still being undertaken for steam locomotives at Swindon Works on 28 May 1961, albeit alongside the construction of replacement diesel hydraulic Type 4s. The last of the thirty-strong County Class designed by Hawksworth to be built was No. 1029 *County of Worcester*, put into service in April 1947. This quick 1961 works visit would see the locomotive out when withdrawn late in 1962. (Frank Hornby)

Rolling stock overhauled at Swindon from the late 1950s would be turned out either in chocolate-and-cream livery for use on prestige expresses and on the Western Region-allocated coaches, or into maroon for other regions as the blood-and-custard scheme fell out of favour. This view from the time shows No. 1019 *County of Merioneth* in very much workaday condition. The county after which it was named was formed in 1284 under the terms of the Statute of Rhuddlan, and once held Dolgellau as its former county town. (Strathwood Library Collection)

At the time of the County Class's introduction there were twenty Class 5800 0-4-2Ts in service; as the 1950s progressed, the class remained intact with many examples still retaining their GWR liveries. By the close of 1957 eleven of the class had been withdrawn that year and, as the end of 1959 approached, which was when this view was taken in the centre roads at Swindon station, just No. 5815 remained in service. Withdrawn in April 1961, it was seen by many visitors to the works dumped out the back with the rest of the scrappers until cut up in the summer of 1964. (Strathwood Library Collection)

Locomotives stabled dead in the sidings adjoining Swindon's Gas Works could be awaiting overhaul, such as in this case with No. 5039 *Rhuddlan Castle* in August 1959; however, for many it would mean something much more sinister as they were destined for cutting up instead! (Late Norman Browne/Strathwood Library Collection)

Sad & Decayed

The first weekend of March 1966 saw four enthusiast specials run over the Somerset & Dorset, utilising nine steam locomotives, a Hymek and a DMU. Used on both days was Battle of Britain Class No. 34057 *Biggin Hill*, seen here at Evercreech Junction; the line closed the following day. (Tony Butcher)

Summer passenger traffic looks brisk at least on 15 June 1963 as passengers transfer to the Western Region's mainline at Highbridge after Collett's 2200 Class 0-6-0 No. 2219 has brought them in off the former Somerset & Dorset Railway's section. The station's porters have thoughtfully brought across two luggage trolleys to help passengers with their belongings, a far cry from rail travel in the twenty-first century! The mainline station would survive the 1966 closures that removed this valuable route across the Mendips. (Peter Simmonds)

The influx of British Railways designed Standards from the late 1950s had started to push out the designs of the former companies, while the transfer of responsibility between the Southern and Western Regions saw neither happy to spend resources on the route. Steam percolates into the cold winter air in early 1965 from underneath Standard Class 4MT No. 80043, as the driver looks back along his rake of Southern coaches while he awaits departure of his stopper away from Bath Green Park. (Edward Dorricott)

We stay at Bath's Green Park station, whose roof fortunately survived the line's closure, for some more activity with British Railway's Standards, as Class 3MT No. 82041 readies to depart with the 11.41 service to Bristol Temple Meads on 11 December 1965. Sadly it looks as though the only passengers today may be enthusiasts taking in the line, as it was posted to close at the year's end. (Douglas Twibble)

It was only the rival bus company's inability or lack of desire to run the replacement bus service that gave the former Somerset & Dorset Railway's route a short reprieve until the beginning of March 1966. That last winter on the line saw this photograph taken at Evercreech Junction, as one service has just left for Bath while Standard Class 4MT No. 80041 awaits the road southwards to Bournemouth with a stopper. (Late Ken Pullen/Strathwood Library Collection)

Severn Bore

One of the large Prairie Class 5101 tanks, No. 4156 leads a Collett Class 2884 2-8-0 out of the Severn Tunnel in 1964 with a lengthy goods train, long before the M4 motorway stole what railway traffic survived the recession of the late 1970s. (Gerald Peacock)

Another cameraman joins us lineside at Caldicot on 17 October 1964, as Standard Class 9F No. 92228 rolls along nicely with a train of coal empties. (Dave Down)

It appears that the second 'C' in the station's nameboard looks to have split and hangs down, appearing to misspell 'Caldicot' the following day. One of the last built of the original Collett-designed Hall Class, No. 6953 *Leighton Hall* looks pretty weary as it makes its way through with a rake of empties. (Dave Down)

The lower quadrant home signal shows up well against the sighting board at the Aust Road catch points protecting the Severn Tunnel in 1964 as a pairing of Classes 7200 and 5101 keep their goods train's couplings stretched out. (Gerald Peacock)

Keeping a sharp lookout, the fireman catches some fresh air as he hangs over the side of one of the modified 2-8-0s with side window cabs, designated 2884 Class, as they pass Blaise near Pilning with an Up freight with No. 2896 in charge. (Gerald Peacock)

Another of these robust locomotives has the double peg at Cattybrook again in 1964, with No. 2891 this time in charge. This would be the last summer for the majority of steam workings through the Severn Tunnel. Through all of the 1950s there were eighty-three of these 2884 Class locomotives in service upon which to call. One was withdrawn during 1962, with further withdrawals during 1963/4 reducing the number of serviceable locomotives to just thirty-four by the start of 1965 – their last year in traffic. (Gerald Peacock)

Western Rover

Starting this round up of Western Region locations, we begin at Cardiff East Dock on 12 July 1964 for a fine portrait of No. 92220 *Evening Star* showing off its lined Brunswick Green livery complete with express headlamps, which was unique for the Class 9F. (Strathwood Library Collection)

Next we go to Pontypool Road on 15 August 1962 as we telephone the signalman for permission to go out on the mainline while Nos 6335, 9611, 3682, 3815 and 4668 are all in view, along with an unknown Class 5600. (Strathwood Library Collection)

The sun is setting on Gloucester shed, coded 85B, in August 1964. Although it remained open to steam until December 1965, the presence of the diesel invasion is being felt, with a newly built Brush Type 4 and a Hymek mingling with the Panniers, Prairies and 4-6-0s. (Win Wall/Strathwood Library Collection)

Doing its best to shroud the shed yard and the turntable at Gloucester Horton Road with its steam was 5101 Class No. 4100, shortly before it was withdrawn in November 1965. (Strathwood Library Collection)

On 13 October 1962 at Neath Riverside, we find a pairing of Panniers, Nos 3706 and 9796, with a train marking the closure of the old Neath & Brecon route for passenger services. This was the second station at this point; opening as the first one closed in 1892, Neath Riverside station finally closed two years after this view. The South Wales mainline crossed the line here on an overbridge just to the right of the photographer. (Strathwood Library Collection)

It's a melancholy task for No. 6931 *Aldborough Hall*, now devoid of its name and number plates on 31 July 1965, which is found passing through Cardiff General dragging Panniers Nos 4663, 4639, 4623 and 5600 Class No. 5655. These were all posted as withdrawn in the previous month and are now on their way for scrapping. The much run-down Hall 4-6-0 would itself succumb to the scrap dealer's tenders that October. (Strathwood Library Collection)

There's a chance for the fireman to get up on the tender and trim his coal before departure from Three Cocks Junction in 1963 on the Swindon-built Mogul, designed by Ivatt for the London, Midland & Scottish Railway, Class 2MT No. 46519. The first of this class of 128 engines went into service from Crewe Works in late 1946, with the last example from here leaving the works in June 1950. Darlington Works then chipped in with the next batch, their first leaving the former North Eastern Railway's workshops in June 1951. By the time that Swindon took over construction in late 1952 until March 1953, the approval for newer designs of Standards, such as Class 4MT 75006, which is seen getting away from Banbury on 23 October 1963, were being favoured. Swindon Works built all eighty of this class of 4-6-0 over a seven-year period from 1951. (Strathwood Library Collection & Michael Beeton)

Most readers will recall the harsh winter of 1963; the snowy conditions drew our cameraman out to Saunderton that February to record another Swindon-built locomotive, No. 48479, which was made again to an LMS design. Meanwhile, the Class 8F heaves another rake of coal empties through the Chilterns for a refill to keep the home fires burning that winter. (John Newman)

We have another view of a Standard Class 9F on the Avonmouth–Bromford Bridge Esso fuel train, as the Crewe Works-built No. 92059 captivates the group of young lads gathered on the platform at Coaley Junction on New Year's Day 1965. (Gilroy Kerr)

Next we are off to enjoy the warm sunshine once more at sleepy Much Wenlock, with Class 2MT No. 41201 rostered for the pick-up in May 1961. Passenger services would cease the following year. This charming station was built between 1860 and 1862, and formed part of the Wellington–Craven Arms Railway's route, which was absorbed into the Great Western Railway. (Strathwood Library Collection)

Another favourite location for photographers was the much busier Bristol–Birmingham mainline at the head of the Lickey bank near Blackwell, where at least one spotter has arrived lineside by bicycle on 27 July 1963 to witness the passing of Standard Class 5MT No. 73094. Notice the smaller calling on arms of the signals for the attentions of the banking engine's crews. (Peter Simmonds)

A healthy extra shove up the Lickey incline near Bromsgrove is being afforded to this goods train from Hawksworth Pannier No. 8418 and Standard Class 9F No. 92079; the latter had taken over from the Midland Railway's Big Bertha 0-10-0 in the mid-1950s. (Strathwood Library Collection)

Trackside gangers work on as No. 6026 *King John* brings the Cambrian Coast Express into Birmingham's Snow Hill station in 1961, oblivious to the hissing of escaping steam at the King's front end. (Strathwood Library Collection)

Passengers would prefer to chat under the awning at Builth Road rather than enjoy the day's sunshine as the fireman of Class 8F No. 48128 climbs up onto the tender while his driver stands ready to let the water flow in 1964. (Strathwood Library Collection)

There is some shunting activity taking place in the shed yard at Worcester on 2 September 1962, as Modified Hall No. 7921 *Edstone Hall* makes its way past one of those distinctive Great Western Railway conical water towers. (Frank Hornby)

Worcester shed was once very proud of its allocation of Castles and looked after them with great care; however, by 27 July 1963, standards have slipped as No. 7023 *Penrice Castle* shuffles about light engine near the station. (Strathwood Library Collection)

Token cleaning has done nothing but highlight the dirt on No. 7011 *Banbury Castle*, simmering in Worcester's shed yard on 7 June 1964 – the glory days have certainly passed now. (Win Wall/Strathwood Library Collection)

The weeds and wild flowers abound as the driver of Pannier No. 8717 sits back and enjoys the sunshine at Berkeley Road before departure to Sharpness in the year before the closure of the branch, which took place in 1964. (Gerald Peacock)

The Great Western's early solution to lightly used branch lines was to introduce diesel railcars, such as this example at Bewdley on 29 August 1959; it seems a few passengers are looking to board this service along the Severn Valley. These were the days when even older lads were happy to wear shorts and long socks in the summer months. (Frank Hornby)

London Division

This was a time when the Modernisation Plan was proposing large fleets of diesel multiple units to take over duties such as this suburban service. It arrived at Paddington from Reading and Slough in 1955 behind large Prairie No. 6106, which was at the head of a rake of red compartment local stock. (Strathwood Library Collection)

Among the headline early duties for the very last of the British Railways Standard Class 9Fs, No. 92220 *Evening Star*, was on the Down Capitals United Express, leaving Paddington at 15.55 for Cardiff on 1 July 1960. At this point the famous last-built steam locomotive was just over three months into its short service career. (Douglas Twibble)

The fireman is busy raking forward what's left of his coal supply on board No. 7928 *Wolf Hall*. The penultimate of the class of seventy-one Modified Halls had begun service in October 1950; by 1964 it still looked clean at least when caught alongside a Hymek at the buffer stops at Paddington. (Strathwood Library Collection)

Clearly just ex-works from Swindon was No. 6016 *King Edward V* when it was photographed on the ash pits at Old Oak Common on 12 November 1961. This overhaul would only have to last until September the following year, with all of its classmates out of traffic soon afterwards. (Strathwood Library Collection)

More and more diesels were invading Old Oak Common's roundhouses every month by the time of this shot in July 1963; the working conditions inside these sheds were far superior to many elsewhere. (Win Wall/ Strathwood Library collection)

The rebuilding of the facilities at Old Oak Common had already begun with the offices by the time this view was taken of No. 6842 *Nunhold Grange* on 15 March 1959. (Strathwood Library Collection)

A large double-sided coaling stage with an equally impressive water tank above it dominated the southern side of the shed yard at Old Oak Common; this ample capacity would be tested at times to keep up with the appetite of not just Castle Class No. 5061 *Earl of Birkenhead*, pictured alongside on 20 September 1959, but also to a massive fleet of Panniers, Prairies, 2-8-0s as well as all those finely named, copper-capped 4-6-0s. (Frank Hornby)

Another of the double-chimney-fitted Castles, built nine years after the example opposite, was No. 7010 *Avondale Castle*, which acquired its new chimney and draughting arrangement only in November 1960. Built in 1948, this was one of thirty-one Castles to emerge from Swindon Works in the reign of British Railways. (Strathwood Library Collection)

Before we take our leave of Old Oak Common, how about another viewing back inside the roundhouses on 21 September 1964 to track down No. 92220 *Evening Star* once again. (Dave Down)

Heading west along the mainline, we arrive at 81C Southall in 1962 to find a far-from-clean No. 4976 *Warfield Hall* being made ready to head a fitted freight westwards. (Strathwood Library Collection)

Some artistic wag has adorned the last built of the Collett Halls, No. 6958 *Oxburgh Hall*, with a set of eyes as it moves slowly off shed early one morning in the cool winter sunshine at 81D Reading in 1964. The Western Region shed would close to steam on 3 January 1965, while the nearby Southern shed had closed beforehand on 6 April 1964. (Bob Treacher/Alton Model Centre)

The driver of No. 5042 *Winchester Castle* has elected to keep his coat on, while his younger fireman, no doubt having been much more energetic with his firing and preparation duties on this cold morning at Reading shed in 1964, is satisfied with his bib and braces. (Bob Treacher/Alton Model Centre)

Shunting some empty stock around the sidings adjoining the station at Didcot keeps 4300 Class Mogul No. 6304 occupied on this occasion in 1959. Built at Swindon Works in late 1920, this locomotive gave good service over a forty-three-year period. Of these machines, 220 joined British Railways in 1948, and they were withdrawn from traffic gradually, with 113 examples still on the books at the end of 1961. Their numbers would half again in the next year, and once more again in both 1962 and 1963, with the last going in 1964, including No. 6304. (Strathwood Library Collection)

Standing on the Down platform at Oxford on 22 April 1959, we can look across to see the driver of Castle Class No. 5071 *Spitfire* taking the opportunity for another oil around before they set off once more. It should be noted that this locomotive was one of the batch of Castles built in 1938, when it was named *Clifford Castle*. In September 1940, it was the first one of twelve of the class to have their names replaced with those of British aircraft familiar to the public during wartime. This fine locomotive, which would have been a great preservation candidate, was cut up by Cooper's Metals at Sharpness in May 1964. (Frank Hornby)

This is a pleasing attempt at trying to keep the black livery clean on large Prairie 6128, which is well beyond the lifespan of this paint scheme, as most of its classmates adopted either lined green or even plain green before they were withdrawn. This was the scene at Oxford in 1962, at a time when only five of the original seventy class members had been withdrawn. (Strathwood Library Collection)

West Country Wanderings

The Western Region once had to share the spoils with the Southern Region or, indeed, the costs of running services around the West Country. One of the many locations where they met with services was here at Barnstaple Junction, where No. 7304 from the 4300 Class stands with a Taunton train on 22 June 1963. (Peter Simmonds)

Having alighted from our train at Taunton, we are in time to see the passage of 'The Devonian' before it was handed over to Warship diesels, although on this day in 1959 it is a scruffy-looking No. 4914 *Cranmore Hall* in charge. (Strathwood Library Collection)

Surely the use of 1400 Class 0-4-2Ts such as No. 1451, captured at Tiverton using autocoaches, was a most practical way of running shuttle or branch line services – this service was certainly threatened when recorded on 22 June 1963, as the following summer the plucky little locomotive was no more. (Peter Simmonds)

A much cleaner example is the subject of our next photograph, taken four years earlier in June 1959, with No. 1468 being prepared for service at Exeter St David's. The presence of the diesel shunter in the background has already made some steam duties redundant. (Alan Pike OBE)

Taken the same day was this shot of Standard Class 9F No. 92204, moving slowly past 83C Exeter shed. The tender alone weighs nearly 14 tons more than the slightly built 1400 Class seen opposite, with the Class 9F locomotive itself packing almost another 87 tons. (Alan Pike OBE)

Continuing our journey westwards to Newton Abbot, we find a dedicated Royal Mail sorting van tucked in behind No. 6921 *Borwick Hall*. The guard stands alongside the cab, no doubt to assist in checking everything was ready for departure along with the platform's porters – such was the way of life in the summer of 1959. (Alan Pike OBE)

A trip along the branch to Kingswear the previous year on 21 July yields more coaching stock in the rather attractive blood-and-custard paint scheme, as No. 4940 *Ludford Hall* draws in. This locomotive was built at Swindon in the early summer of 1929, and it would unfortunately be withdrawn before the dawn of the 1960s, being taken out of traffic in November 1959 and cut up the following month. (Strathwood Library Collection)

Back to our summer holidays once more as we spend some time with the family on the beach at Coryton Cove on 20 July 1961. Our attention is drawn towards the exhaust of the passing Hall Class 4-6-0, which is heading westwards, no doubt with more holiday makers and day trippers on board. (Alan Pike OBE)

Let's get into the holiday spirit and take a boat trip around the cove at Dawlish on this nice day in the summer of 1959. The arrival of DMUs has yet to send the use of Prairie tanks on the local services into history and we can take this lovely shot as a fond reminder of the day. (Alan Pike OBE)

Many enthusiasts were attracted to the branch to Hemyock for the picturesque nature of the stations and the use of mixed trains transferring the milk tankers to and from the dairy just past the terminus. In the last summer of steam operation in 1963, we find No. 1421 on duty for today's shunting at the dairy. (Strathwood Library Collection)

On 2 May 1959 there were very few diesel hydraulics available for the mainline services through Plymouth North Road, and so it would appear that No. 6824 *Ashley Grange* may well have a good few years' life left in her on that day. Indeed the first casualty within the eighty-strong class would only come in 1960; just nine had fallen by the end of 1963, but the next two years would send every remaining one of them to the scrapyard. (Frank Hornby)

Plymouth was also a regular host to Southern Region types, not just on the metals of the former London & South Western Railway but also at the city's Laira shed, which is where N Class No. 31843 was catching the winter sunshine by the coaling stage on 14 December 1963. Very few signs of her lined black livery show through the muck. (Dave Down)

On 3 May 1964, West Country Class No. 34002 *Salisbury* brings 'The Cornubian' special off the Saltash Bridge and into the station. This RCTS and Plymouth Railway Circle tour was run to mark the passing of steam on the Cornish mainline. Even with a relatively light load, No. 34002's running was impressive, and the Plymouth crew were pleased by the performance of their first and most likely only run with such a Pacific. (Dave Down)

This is a delightful shot from May 1959 of the Saltash rail motor from Plymouth in the hands of one the 6400 Class Panniers, which were used before the service went over to DMU working on 13 June 1960. (Strathwood Library Collection)

It's an overcast day on 7 June 1961 in the sidings at Looe, and 4575 Class Prairie Tank No. 5518 certainly doesn't have a lot to handle today. Fortunately the branch survives on passenger revenue alone these days. (Phil Nunn Collection)

We are 299 miles from the bufferstops at Paddington on the platforms here at St Erth in September 1959, as No. 1002 *County of Berks* makes an early stop in its long journey towards the capital from Penzance. (Late Norman Browne/Strathwood Library Collection)

Specials

On 31 July 1965, the Swansea Railway Circle ran their 'Rambling 56' special behind 5600 Class No. 6643, which operated throughout on a tour of the valleys, as here at the now-closed Taff & Bargoed Joint Railway station at Bedlinog. (Strathwood Library Collection)

The Railway Enthusiasts' Club arranged a brake van tour around the Wrexham area on 17 July 1965, hauled by No. 4683; they called their train 'The Flintstone Special'. (Chris Forest)

On the SLS-arranged Severn & Wye District Tour of 13 May 1961, passenger comfort was much improved with three autocoaches utilising two Panniers, Nos 6437 and 8701, seen here at Coleford. (Strathwood Library Collection)

As can be seen in this view of the special on the same day, the auto-fitted No. 6437 was utilised within the autocoaches, as the ensemble passed the Northern United Colliery in the Forest of Dean at around 15.30. The tour started and finished at Gloucester Central. (Strathwood Library Collection)

The LCGB arranged 'The Western Ranger Tour' on 15 August 1965. Interestingly, this ran out and back from the Southern Region's Waterloo terminus. After taking in Swindon Works behind No. 3863, which had taken over from No. 75066 at Reading General, the baton was handed over here at Radley to No. 9773 for the train to take a run around the Oxfordshire branches. (Strathwood Library Collection)

The weather was suitably miserable for the LCGB's 'The King Commerative Rail Tour', which was run on 17 November 1962 behind 6018 No. *King Henry VI*, seen here at Birmingham Snow Hill. The outward route was from Paddington via Princes Risborough behind the 'King' to Wolverhampton Low Level. Here 5600 Class No. 6631 was waiting to take the tour onwards to Leamington Spa where a change to one of Collett's 0-6-0s, No. 2210, took the passengers back to London Marylebone across country to gain the former Great Central mainline. (Late Vincent Heckford/Strathwood Library Collection)

Another interesting trip was undertaken behind No. 7029 *Clun Castle* on 3 April 1965, starting from Birmingham Snow Hill with a run towards London via High Wycombe to take the Greenford curve, and back towards Maidenhead, where this stop was made, before heading for Swindon Works. After the works visit the tour participants entrained once more behind the Castle towards Didcot for the curve, taking them back northwards to Oxford and on to Kings Norton, where steam was exchanged for D5226 to take the run under the wires into New Street. (Edward Dorricott)

Enthusiasts' tours in the early 1960s were so interesting, as they were arranged so as to take in as many threatened routes as they could along with as many surviving steam locomotive types as they could conjure up. One such example was with the LCGB's 'Thames, Avon and Severn Rail Tour' on 12 October 1963; we see it here at Stratford Old Town with Nos 6368 and 2246 in charge, but No. 7005 *Sir Edward Elgar*, the preserved T9 120, No. 31790, No. 45552 *Silver Jubilee*, No. 82023 and No. 92223 all did their bit on the day. (Strathwood Library Collection)

However, some tours just could not be run with the luxury of such motive power due to weight restrictions, as in this instance near Princess Royal Colliery in the Forest of Dean on 20 June 1964. Tour participants enjoyed a wide-ranging tour of these freight routes in brake vans instead, hauled behind both Nos 1658 and 1664, seen here. The tour was called the 'Severn Boar II' and was a repeat running of the same tour a fortnight earlier, such was the demand for tickets. (Strathwood Library Collection)

Above and previous page: The two favoured Castles, Nos 4079 *Pendennis Castle* and 7029 *Clun Castle*, were much used at this time for enthusiasts' specials, such as in this case, with the former at the head of an Ian Allan jaunt from Paddington to Worcester and back via both the Oxford and Swindon routes on 8 August 1965. Then, to commemorate the 'Farewell to Steam on the Western Region' on 27 November 1965, *Clun Castle* was selected. We see it at Bristol Temple Meads, but D1006 *Western Stalwart* and D6881 with D6882 ran legs as well unfortunately. It seems several parents took their offspring to witness what might have been their last glimpse of a live steam engine that day. (Both: Strathwood Library Collection)

Thankfully it was not the end of Western steam on the mainlines, as two specials were run on 4 March 1967, when Ian Allan arranged for 'The Birkenhead Flyer' with No. 4079 *Pendennis Castle* and 'The Zulu' with No. 7029 *Clun Castle*. Both specials are seen here at Chester while the trains went on to Birkenhead and back behind Nos 73035 and 73026 respectively. *Clun* worked her special from Didcot to here and then back to Birmingham Snow Hill, while Pendennis took over at Didcot and returned her special back there from Chester. It was hydraulic power with a Hymek and a Western that were used for both legs out and also back from Paddington. (Strathwood Library Collection & Tony Butcher)

As we have seen already, a number of locomotives were repainted with their traditional style of numbering on the bufferbeams in true Great Western flair. Another of these to catch our eye was No. 1011 *County of Chester*, which is with a special near Abbotswood Junction on 20 September 1964 to bid farewell to the County Class. It ran out and back from Birmingham Snow Hill to Swindon on a circular route, out via Gloucester and Kemble, and then on the return back via Didcot, Oxford and Leamington Spa. (Strathwood Library Collection)

Bristol Shiftwork

It's chocolate-and-cream stock for the 'Devonian' but this time with a filthy Jubilee, No. 45662 *Kempenfelt*, at Bristol Temple Meads in 1962. This service's title was a bit of misnomer for many years, as, outside of the summer months, the service did not go Devon at all; instead, it ran between Bradford and Bristol. It was only extended to Torquay and Paignton in the warmer months for the benefit of holidaymakers. (Gerald Peacock)

Armed with a powerful flash gun, our intrepid cameraman captured a number of views at Bristol Temple Meads after dark, as here with No. 45658 *Keyes* on 1 August 1964 with the night mail. (Dave Down)

Several weeks later on 25 September, it befell No. 6820 *Kingstone Grange* to act as the standby locomotive should it be needed at Temple Meads, and for any shunting requirements during the shift. (Dave Down)

Back to August 1964, and Black Five No. 45417 has paused at Temple Meads long enough for another shot to be grabbed with the flash. Then again the same year on 26 September it is the turn of Britannia No. 70001 *Lord Hurcomb*, with what looks like the same crew rostered for this turn. (Both: Dave Down)

The Temple Meads station pilot on 18 August 1964 was Class 4F No. 44135, supplied from Bristol's Barrow Road shed in the last months of its thirty-nine years of service. The crew look pretty relaxed as they await instructions from control. (Dave Down)

We close our night shift at the city's St Philip's Marsh shed in 1962, with some disposal and preparation duties now that the sun has come up again. 1361 Class No. 1365 is taking on water this morning; it would be the last one of her class to be scrapped in September 1963. (Gerald Peacock)

Swindon's Bone Yard

Just in case their tenders could find further use, they have been all been removed from this line-up on death row at Swindon in the summer of 1962. The line includes large Prairie No. 6157, which had been withdrawn in May and would perish here by that September. It should also be noted that many of the condemned still carry their name and number plates. (John Gill)

Awaiting its destiny in front of the cutting staff on 18 October 1959, just a few weeks after being withdrawn, was No. 7743. It would soon be moved into position from the sidings adjoining the gas works, however, as it was cut up in January 1960. (Frank Hornby)

The reign of No. 6025 *King Henry III* was soon to end at Swindon in March 1964. It had been withdrawn from service in December 1962 and, after languishing on death row, its final disposal would take place two months after this shot was taken. (Late Norman Browne/Strathwood Library Collection)

Fellow enthusiasts take the numbers of what they can as they pass along the lines in Swindon's scrapping area on 12 August 1962. This task is made easier on No. 5682 as the smokebox number plate has yet to be removed. One cannot but wonder whether this now-valuable souvenir survived to fall into the hands of collectors? (Frank Hornby)

On 26 March 1961, a small party are again making their way, this time around the gas works sidings, in search of what awaits entry to the works, including No. 1652. The lightweight 1600 Class Pannier had been withdrawn in January 1960; ironically it had been built here at Swindon Works just five years beforehand in December 1954, and it would perish here too in July 1961. (Strathwood Library Collection)

Conversely, the story of the Churchward-designed No. 2818 would tell us that it was built here at Swindon Works in December 1905, giving valuable service until withdrawn in October 1963. It was then kept in the yard alongside less fortunate classmates such as No. 3855, as here on 3 April 1965. Further irony was that it would then be the works of the Southern Region at Eastleigh that would be given the task of restoring No. 2818 as part of the National Collection in 1966. (Edward Dorricott)

The partly cut boilers from at least five pannier tanks were also to be found on that same visit to Swindon Works on 3 April 1965, with the clever use of a redundant bridge allowing the boilers to be supported while they are cut up. (Edward Dorricott)

Enthusiasts are here again on 24 July 1964, inspecting the locomotives awaiting disposal, including No. 9420 at the front of the line. She would be gone within days now, with her remains no doubt sent to the hungry steel furnaces of South Wales for re-use. (Frank Hornby)

Preservation Movements

Happily, from all this carnage of the steam fleet, some examples were chosen to survive for preservation, such as the Great Western Society's No. 1466, seen shuffling alongside the mainline at Cholsey on 21 September 1968. (Strathwood Library Collection)

In pretty much original condition and restored for display in the Science Museum was No. 4073 *Caerphilly Castle*, awaiting transfer to Kensington by Pickfords' low loaders. It waits inside the carriage sheds at Old Oak Common in June 1961; the loading took place at Park Royal. (Strathwood Library Collection)

Back to the activities of the Great Western Society once more to enjoy No. 7808 *Cookham Manor* at an estimated 80 mph on the approaches to West Ruislip on 17 September 1966. The tour was from Birmingham Snow Hill and back to allow the Manor to appear at the Open Day being held at Taplow. (Aldo Delicata)

Now preserved and safe from the cutters was the resplendent (externally, at least) No. 4079 *Pendennis Castle*, which is seen coming off shed at Southall during 1965, complete with Great Western lettering once more. The controversial export to West Australia was yet to come! (Strathwood Library Collection)

The task of delivering this pairing of Nos 3205 and 4555 to the Dart Valley Railway at Totnes was undertaken in connection with a special from Paddington, using No. 4079 *Pendennis Castle* and Warship D841 *Roebuck*. We see the duo heading for Totnes from Exeter St David's on 2 October 1965. (Dave Down)

An early Great Western preservation candidate was No. 3440 *City of Truro*, storming through Theale on its way to Bristol via Trowbridge, having taken over this tour from No. 30453 *King Arthur* at Reading General on 28 April 1957. (Aldo Delicata)

Cambrian Adventures

The overall roof at Shrewsbury was already in the process of being dismantled when this shot of No. 1025 *County of Radnor* was recorded in May 1962. It looks as though there are a good number of spotters on hand as it's the Whitsun holidays. A few weeks beforehand, the BRCW-built prototype D0260 *Lion* was visiting here on trials, just as No. 6964 *Thornbridge Hall* was bringing the Cambrian Coast Express through the town. (Both: Strathwood Library Collection)

A reasonably clean No. 2859, still fresh from its last works visit, was seen making its way around the yards at Shrewsbury in 1962 between freight workings. (Strathwood Library Collection)

One of the self-weighing tenders is attached to Black Five No. 45298 as it gets away from Llantwythd Wells with a Shrewsbury service on a glorious 13 July 1963. (Peter Simmonds)

Also noted on the same sunny day at Llantwythd Wells with a Swansea train was No. 73095. (Peter Simmonds)

One of the many Cambrian Coast regulars was No. 7819 *Hinton Manor*, seen at Shrewsbury in 1963. (Strathwood Library Collection)

Taken the same day was this shot of the smartened-up No. 7803 *Barcote Manor*, again at Shrewsbury. (Strathwood Library Collection)

The meeting of the Talyllyn line with *Edward Thomas* at the bufferstops compares with the standard gauge bulk of No. 75009, waiting in the exchange siding in August 1966 at Towyn. (Edward Dorricott)

It's a stop-off at Oswestry next in 1963 to await the departure of No. 7812 *Erlestoke Manor*. (Strathwood Library Collection)

It looks like a good number of passengers have just alighted from the Gobowen train at Oswestry that No. 1458 has just propelled in on 20 July 1963. (Peter Simmonds)

Taken on the same trip on 20 July 1963, our cameraman is hurried along as they want to get Standard 3MT No. 82031 back on its way to Carmarthen from Tregavron. (Peter Simmonds)

Passengers only just outnumber the platform staff at Dolgellau as Standard Class 4MT No. 75006 arrives in 1963. (Strathwood Library Collection)

The summer of 1963 was a fabulous time to explore the Cambrian section, as we see Standard 4MT No. 80105 piloting No. 7820 *Dinmore Manor* away from Machynclleth with the Shrewsbury-bound Cambrian Coast Express on 20 July. Our cameraman was on hand again on the same day to record No. 7810 *Draycott Manor* picking up the staff at Lampeter while in charge of a Carmarthan train. (Both: Peter Simmonds)

The evening mail train was the duty of No. 7810 *Draycott Manor* two months later in September the same year at Dovey Junction. (Edward Dorricott)

There was more activity at Dovey Junction two years beforehand as No. 7827 *Lydham Manor* awaited onward movement and Standard Class 3MT No. 82021 started to blow at her safety valves on the other line. (Strathwood Library Collection)

The Vale of Rheidol trio are all picked up at Aberystwyth. Firstly there was No. 7 *Owain Glyndwr* in 1956, and then No. 8 *Llywelyn* two years later and, finally, on 8 June 1963 to bag No. 9 *Prince of Wales* being coaled at the original narrow-gauge shed. (Strathwood Library Collection & Frank Hornby)

In this pleasant view across Barmouth's waterfront, what looks like a Dukedog gets away in 1956. During the 1950s the deliveries of both Ivatt and Riddles 2MT Moguls sent the Dukedogs to the scrapmen on the lightly laid Cambrian section, where we meet No. 46446 of the Ivatt design in 1963. (Both: Strathwood Library Collection)

Specials were run in the early days for members to travel to the Ffestiniog Railway Society's AGM. These involved pairs of Dukedogs initially; however, by the time of the 1960 meeting on 30 April, they were almost extinct. As a result No. 7827 *Lydham Manor* was provided as the pilot to No. 9021 when the pair stopped for water at Barmouth. The duo took over at Ruabon for the run to Minffordd and back. No. 1019 *County of Merioneth* had been requested, as the Ffestiniog Railway is situated in what was then the namesake's county, but in the event the train was taken by No. 1021 *County of Montgomery* for the Paddington–Ruabon and return legs. (Craig McBrine Collection)

We take our leave of the Cambrian section, with Standard Class 4MT No. 75012 passing one of the tank engine versions of the same power classification at Barmouth in 1964. (Strathwood Library Collection)

Interlopers

Another Ian Allan-arranged special, on 1 September 1964, brought No. 46245 *City of London* to Paddington for a run to allow spotters to visit Crewe Works, going out via Birmingham Snow Hill and Shrewsbury. (Strathwood Library Collection)

We have seen Western Region specials starting from the Southern Region – how about one going the other way instead? On 12 October 1958, we find Class E1 No. 31019 ready to depart Paddington for Kent! (Strathwood Library Collection)

Or perhaps a tender-first freight working for nicely presented No. 46101 *Royal Scots Grey*, near Old Oak Common on 22 October 1962. (Strathwood Library Collection)

Final preparations are well in hand at 81C Southall for Class A4 No. 60007 *Sir Nigel Gresley* to make its return run to Manchester Exchange from Paddington on 23 October 1965, in charge of the 'Paddington Streamliner Railtour', raising funds for the A4 Preservation Society. (Strathwood Library Collection)

In the 1960s, Swindon Works carried out several light overhauls on Ivatt Class 4MTs such as No. 43047, seen awaiting the journey home to the London Midland Region outside 82C Swindon's running shed in August 1964. (Late Norman Browne/Strathwood Library Collection)

Here's another Southern Region locomotive starting a tour from the Western Region; this time it's No. 34051 *Winston Churchill*, leaving Banbury on 23 May 1965. Having started the train from Birmingham Snow Hill, it was heading for the next changeover at Salisbury. (Strathwood Library Collection)

This time it's No. 4472 *Flying Scotsman*, approaching King's Sutton with the 'Farnborough Flyer' tour for the air show, starting from Sheffield, which it worked as far as Basingstoke, where No. 34037 *Clovelly* was on hand. The tour was arranged by the famous A3's owner, the late Alan Pegler, for 12 September 1964. (Strathwood Library Collection)

On 24 June 1962 it was the turn of No. 30850 *Lord Nelson* to visit Swindon for a works and a shed visit for the Home Counties Railway Club. The opportunity was also taken to visit the newly opened Great Western Railway Museum, which opened its doors two days beforehand. (Strathwood Library Collection)

Ex-Works Swindon

There is no lining, sadly, but at least a coat of fresh green paint for 4300 Class No. 7340 on 28 May 1961. This locomotive had been originally numbered as 9318 when built at Swindon in April 1932, taking on this new number in December 1957. (Frank Hornby)

The Great Western Railway built their 4200 Class 2-8-0T locomotives to the design of Churchward between 1910 and 1923. They were designed for short-haul coal trips from coal mines to ports in South Wales, working the heaviest coal trains through the Welsh valleys. The locomotives were built with large boilers and narrow side tanks; they were to have been designed to be capable of passing numerous water stops along their routes. However, because of the class's heavy water consumption and limited tank capacity to feed such a large boiler, they were nicknamed 'Water Carts'. Many of the lines in South Wales had sharp curves and to traverse these curves the locomotives were constructed with side play in the trailing driving wheels and coupling rods, with spherical joints to allow for movement in any direction. The later build of 5205 Class were very similar, although some were to be rebuilt in the form of 2-8-2Ts and classified as the 7200 Class. Standing outside Swindon's famous works on 8 February 1960 ready for a return to traffic until it was withdrawn in October 1963 was No. 4257. (Frank Hornby)

The plain and sometimes lined black liveries for the Prairie tank fleet had given way to the application of the more pleasing lined green, as applied to No. 5182 outside the works in the sunshine on 20 September 1959. However, this would not last, as the final overhauls for such engines were sending them back out in plain lined green, as we witness on No. 6167, ready to go back into traffic, on 11 May 1963 outside the works. (Both: Strathwood Library Collection)

There was a much higher standard of finish given to Standard Class 5MT No. 73093 on 8 March 1964, in lined black livery. It awaits being reunited with its tender, upon which testing can take place and the locomotive can be signed back off the works into traffic once more. (Dave Down)

Final tinkering needs to be completed on Standard Class 4MT No. 75008 by the works turntable in 1962, as the locomotive was destined for a return to traffic on the Western Region. Swindon's painters have gone to town on a splendid lined green livery instead. (Strathwood Library Collection)

For one of the Hawksworth-designed 9400 Class, the painters have left the copper chimney cap polished, but have elected to paint the brass safety valve cowl black, as she awaits release again on 24 March 1963. (Frank Hornby)

Running in on one of the local stoppers was the trip of choice for many an ex-works 4-6-0 from Swindon, with No. 6007 *King William III* ready to follow this pattern during 1961 as it waits at Swindon station. (John Gill)

The temptation to take a look in the cab is there for one enthusiast at Swindon on 9 April 1961, as No. 4902 *Aldenham Hall* waits for release from the works. (Frank Hornby)

Both the North British-built Warship D833 *Panther*, which has arrived for light repairs, and Standard Class 4MT No. 76037 will soon go back into service after this visit on 12 June 1964. (Peter Coton)

When construction of British Railways steam locomotives ended with No. 92220 *Evening Star* in 1960, it was firstly the construction of the last of the Warships, then a batch of Westerns and finally the wasteful D9500 series of 0-6-0s that shared the main workshops, with this Standard Class 9F and a Grange both in for overhauls. We all perhaps prefer to remember Swindon for ex-works lined-green 4-6-0s such as No. 4914 *Cranmore Hall*, which is at the nearby running shed in 1960 in front of a likewise magnificent Castle. (Strathwood Library Collection & Richard Icke)